D0845547

Hawaii

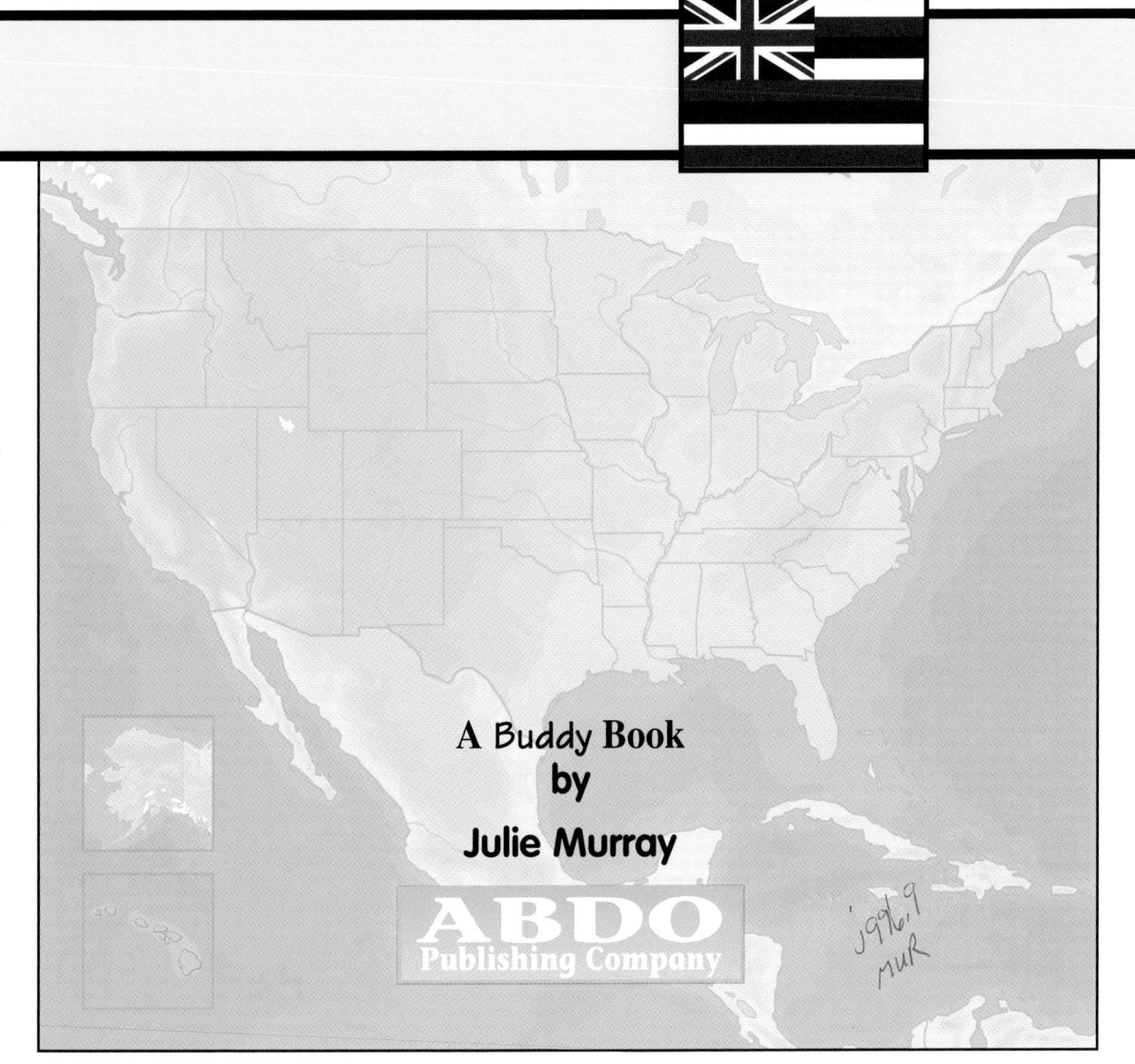

A Buddy Book
by
Julie Murray

ABDO
Publishing Company

j996.9
MUR

PH EK BB DG

VISIT US AT
www.abdopub.com

Published by ABDO Publishing Company, 4940 Viking Drive, Edina, Minnesota 55435.

Copyright © 2006 by Abdo Consulting Group, Inc. International copyrights reserved in all countries. No part of this book may be reproduced in any form without written permission from the publisher. Buddy Books™ is a trademark and logo of ABDO Publishing Company.

Printed in the United States.

Edited by: Sarah Tieck
Contributing Editor: Michael P. Goecke
Graphic Design: Deb Coldiron, Maria Hosley
Image Research: Sarah Tieck
Photographs: Clipart.com, Corbis, Getty Images, One Mile Up, PhotoDisc, Photos.com

Library of Congress Cataloging-in-Publication Data

Murray, Julie, 1969-
    Hawaii / Julie Murray.
        p. cm. — (The United States)
    Includes bibliographical references and index.
    ISBN 1-59197-670-7
        1. Hawaii—Juvenile literature. I. Title.

DU623.25.M87 2005
996.9—dc22

                                                        2004054453

Table Of Contents

A Snapshot Of Hawaii

Hawaii is the only state in the United States that is not on the continent of North America. It is made up of 132 islands. Hawaii is far from any other land. The only way to visit Hawaii is to travel by airplane or boat.

Hawaii has palm trees.

People wear leis in Hawaii. Leis are necklaces made of flowers. They are a sign of welcome.

Hawaiians greet visitors with a lei. Many people wear leis at luaus, or Hawaiian feasts. At a luau, people eat pig, fish, and chicken. Some people do a Hawaiian dance called the hula. Dancers move their hips and arms as they tell a story about the islands.

Some people surf in Hawaii.

There are 50 states in the United States. Every state is different. Every state has an official state nickname. Hawaii is known as the "Aloha State." When you visit Hawaii, you are sure to hear people say "Aloha." Aloha is a Hawaiian word that means hello, welcome, love, and good-bye.

After years of being ruled by a Hawaiian king, Hawaii became a United States territory in 1900. Hawaii was the last state to join the United States. It became the 50th state on August 21, 1959.

Hawaii has 6,459 square miles (16,729 sq km) of land. It is the fourth-smallest state in the United States. Only Delaware, Connecticut, and Rhode Island are smaller. Hawaii is home to 1,211,537 people.

People visit Waikiki
Beach in Hawaii.

Where Is Hawaii?

There are four parts of the United States. Each part is called a region. Each region is in a different area of the country. The United States Census Bureau says the four regions are the Northeast, the South, the Midwest, and the West.

Hawaii is in the West region of the United States. Hawaii has mild weather. It is warm all year.

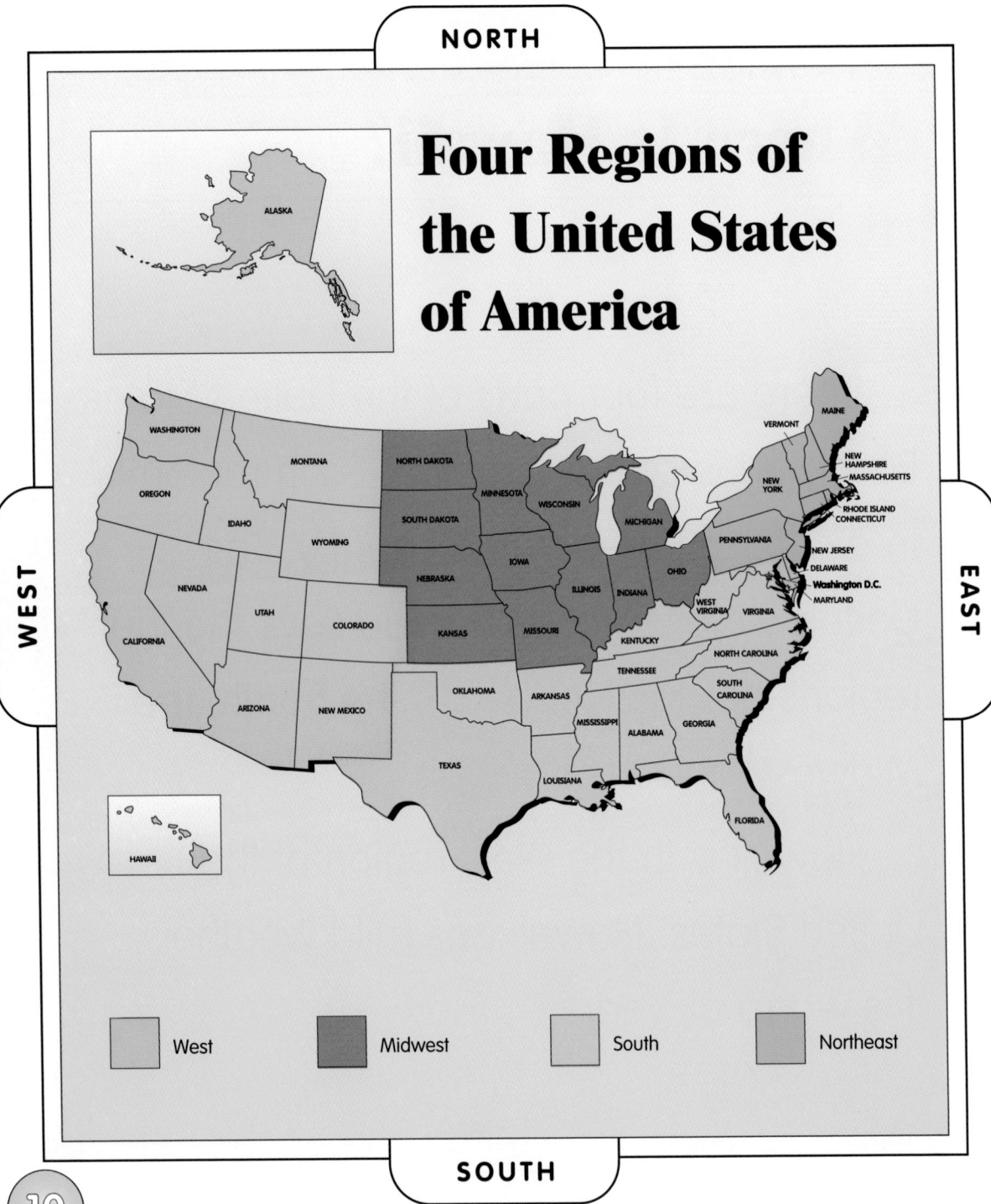

Four Regions of the United States of America

NORTH

WEST

EAST

SOUTH

West Midwest South Northeast

10

Hawaii is not bordered by any other states. It is a chain of islands located in the middle of the Pacific Ocean. Islands are surrounded by water. Hawaii is made up of 132 islands. Eight of these are main islands. The other 124 islands are very small and some of them are barely above sea level.

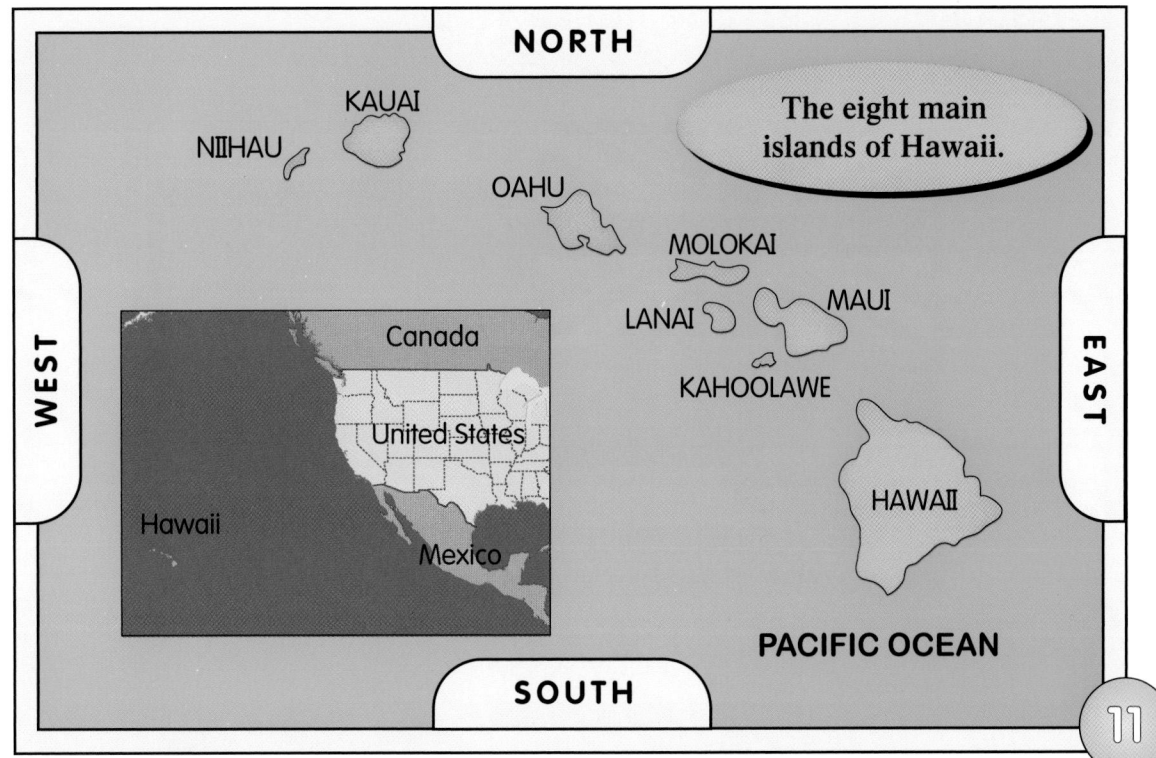

NORTH

KAUAI

NIIHAU

The eight main islands of Hawaii.

OAHU

MOLOKAI

MAUI

LANAI

KAHOOLAWE

WEST

EAST

Canada

United States

Hawaii

Mexico

HAWAII

PACIFIC OCEAN

SOUTH

Hawaii

State abbreviation: HI

State nickname: The Aloha State

State capital: Honolulu

State motto: *Ua Mau ke Ea o Ka Aina i ka Pono*
(Hawaiian for "The Life of the Land is
Perpetuated in Righteousness")

Statehood: August 21, 1959, 50th state

Population: 1,211,537, ranks 42nd

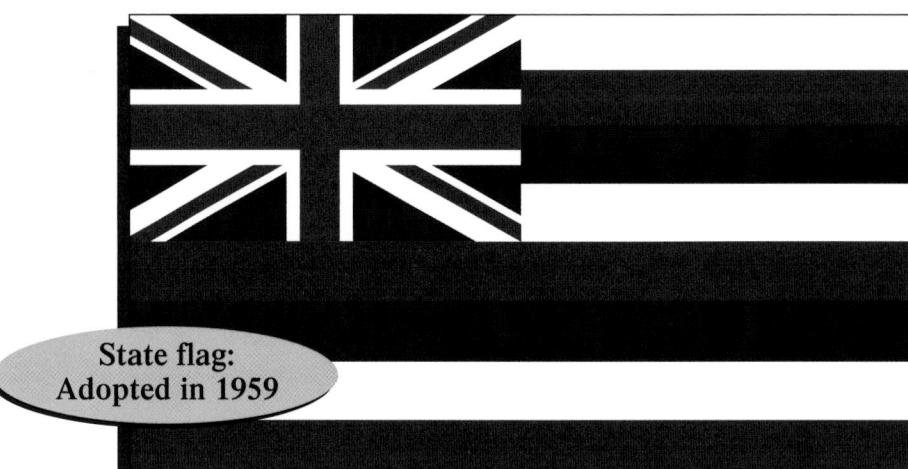

State flag:
Adopted in 1959

Land area: 6,459 square miles (16,729 sq km), ranks 47th

State tree: Kukui (candlenut tree)

State song: "Hawaii Ponoi" ("Hawaii's Own")

State government: Three branches: legislative, executive, and judicial

Average July temperature: 75°F (24°C)

Average January temperature: 68°F (20°C)

State flower: Yellow hibiscus

State bird: Nene (Hawaiian goose)

State marine mammal: Humpback whale

Cities And The Capital

Honolulu is Hawaii's capital and largest city. It is on the island of Oahu. Oahu is the largest and most populated island in the state. Many people come to Honolulu for vacations. Honolulu also has a number of business and military bases. Some people call it "The Crossroads of the Pacific."

The skyline of Honolulu.

Hilo is Hawaii's second-largest city. It is also the largest city on the island of Hawaii, often called the "Big Island." Hilo is located on Hilo Bay, near Kilauea, one of Hawaii's active volcanoes. Some of the products of Hilo include orchids, guava, ginger, and macadamia nuts.

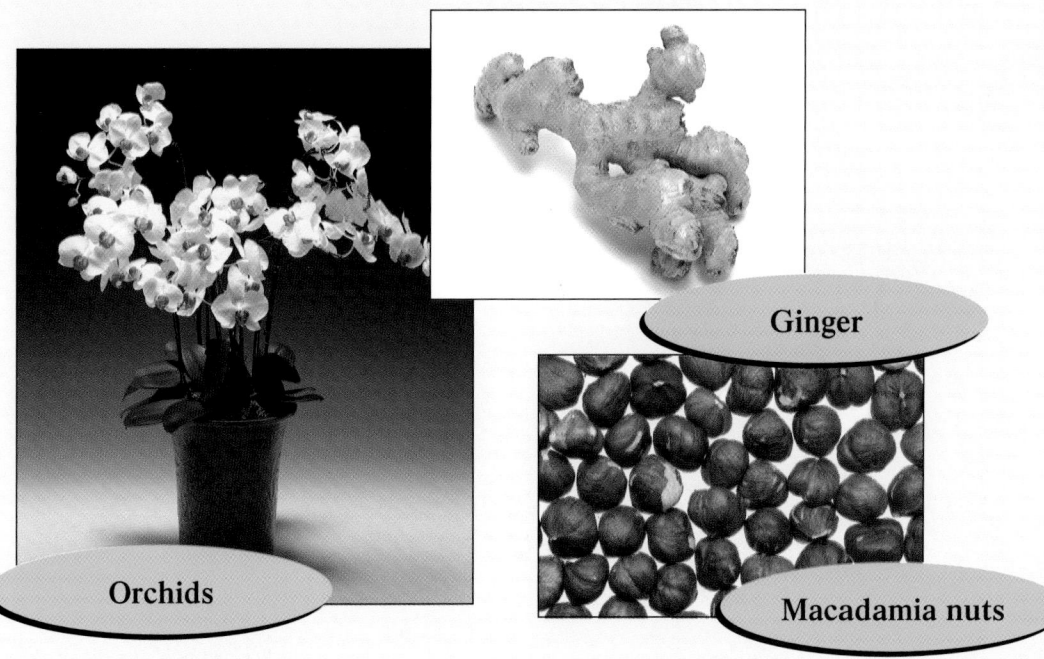

Ginger

Orchids

Macadamia nuts

Famous Citizens

Lydia Kamekeha Liliuokalani (1838-1917)

Lydia Kamekeha Liliuokalani was born in Honolulu. She is famous for being the last queen of Hawaii. Hawaii is the only state that was a small nation with its own monarchy. Queen Liliuokalani reigned from 1891 to 1893.

Queen Liliuokalani

She lost her throne when settlers from the United States revolted. She is also remembered for a song called "Aloha Oe." Many people know this as Hawaii's good-bye song.

Famous Citizens

Reverend Joseph Damien de Veuster (1840-1889)

Joseph Damien de Veuster was born in Belgium. But, he spent many years of his life helping sick people on one of Hawaii's islands. He was known as Father Damien to the people of Molokai. Many people on Molokai had a sickness called leprosy. Some even died from leprosy. Healthy people were afraid they would catch leprosy. Father Damien was healthy, but he helped the sick people of Molokai. This made him a hero.

People of Molokai

Humpback Whales

Humpback whales are the state marine mammal of Hawaii. In the winter months, some humpback whales come to Hawaii to have their babies. Whale babies are called calves.

Humpback whales are huge. They usually weigh about 29 tons (26 t). These whales can grow over 45 feet (14 m) long.

Humpback whales swim in
all oceans of the world.

Humpback whales have two flippers that help them when swimming.

Humpback whales are black on the top and white on the bottom. All whales have blowholes. The humpback whale has two blowholes on top of its head. Whales take in air and let it out through their blowholes.

Pearl Harbor

Pearl Harbor is a naval base. It is located in southern Oahu. In the early 1900s, the United States Navy created a base at Pearl Harbor.

Pearl Harbor became famous in 1941. On December 7, 1941, Japanese planes attacked the United States ships at Pearl Harbor. Many American planes and warships were destroyed during the attack at Pearl Harbor. More than 2,300 people died, and 2,000 people were injured. Because of this attack, America went to war against Japan and other countries in World War II.

Visitors can still visit the site of this battle. There is a memorial for the U.S.S. *Arizona*. The U.S.S. *Arizona* was a ship that sank during the attack on Pearl Harbor. Many of the men on that ship died in the attack. It is called the U.S.S. *Arizona* Memorial. They can also visit the Battleship *Missouri* Memorial.

Today, Pearl Harbor is still home to a United States Naval Base. It is called Pearl Harbor Naval Complex.

U.S.S. *Arizona* Memorial

Volcanoes Of Hawaii

The islands of Hawaii were created by volcanic lava. Over millions and millions of years, volcanoes erupted on the ocean floor. Hot lava was cooled by the water and hardened. The lava continued to grow until it rose up out of the ocean water like a mountain.

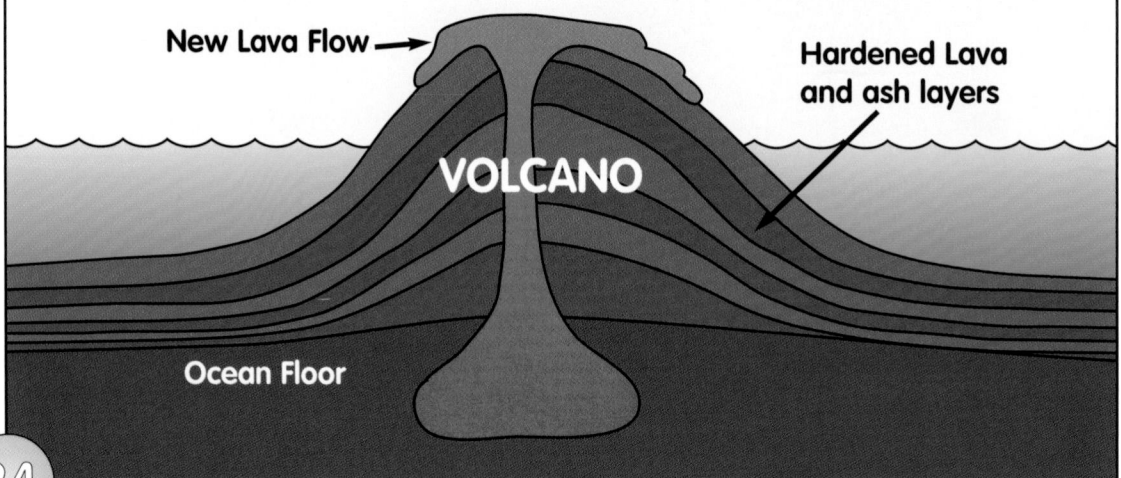

New Lava Flow ➔

Hardened Lava and ash layers

VOLCANO

Ocean Floor

Hot lava flows out of volcanoes when they erupt.

Many people visit Hawaii's beaches.

Today, the islands are lush and tropical. There are caves, rain forests, and sandy beaches. The volcano peaks look like hills and mountains. Some are high enough to get snow in the winter. People even ski on inactive volcanoes during the winter months.

There are many inactive volcanoes in Hawaii.

There are two active volcanoes found on the island of Hawaii. They are called Kilauea and Mauna Loa. They are both located in Hawaii Volcanoes National Park. People can get close to see the volcanoes. Some people call Kilauea the "drive-in volcano" because people can get so close to it.

Hawaii

1778: Captain James Cook arrives in Hawaii.

1810: Hawaii's islands become one kingdom. King Kamehameha is the first king.

1885: People in Hawaii start growing pineapple.

1900: Hawaii becomes a United States territory.

1934: Franklin Roosevelt visits Hawaii. He is the first president to visit the islands.

A statue of King Kamehameha.

Pineapple is a tropical fruit. It is grown in Hawaii.

1941: Pearl Harbor is bombed on December 7.

1946: A tsunami wave hits Hilo.

1959: Hawaii becomes the 50th state.

1969: The television show *Hawaii Five-O* starts filming in Hawaii.

1983: Kilauea volcano erupts on Hawaii.

Steam rises from Kilauea volcano.

1987: John Waihee is the first U.S. governor of Hawaiian descent.

1992: Hurricane Iniki damages Kauai and Oahu.

2002: Linda Lingle is the first woman governor of Hawaii.

Islands and Cities in Hawaii

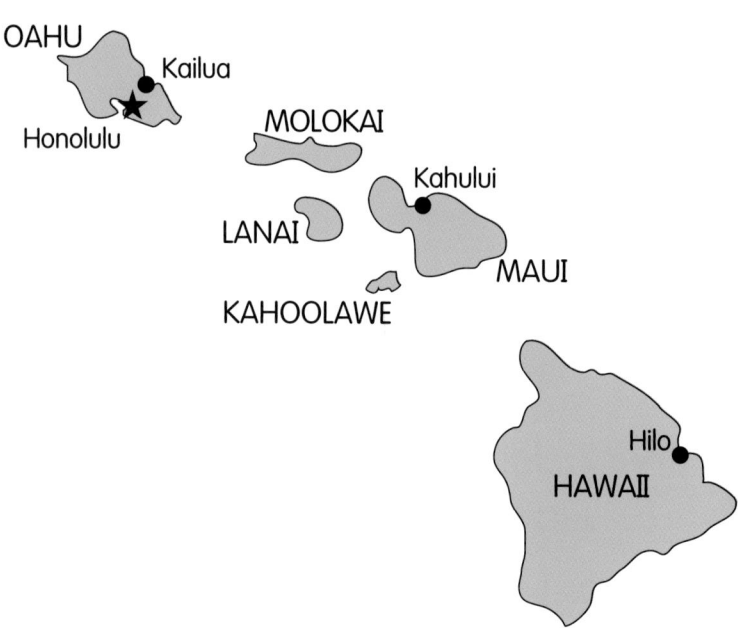

KAUAI

NIIHAU

OAHU

Kailua

Honolulu

MOLOKAI

Kahului

LANAI

MAUI

KAHOOLAWE

Hilo

HAWAII

Important Words

capital a city where government leaders meet.

continent one of the earth's seven main land areas.

island a piece of land surrounded by water.

lava hot liquid that flows from a volcano.

leprosy a sickness that affects the skin and can spread to other people. For many years, people were afraid of people with leprosy. They made them live in separate places.

mammal most living things that belong to this special group have hair, give birth to live babies, and make milk to feed their babies.

monarchy a country that is ruled by a king or a queen.

nickname a name that describes something special about a person or a place.

revolt rising up against the government.

World War II the second war between many countries that happened from 1939–1945.

Web Sites

To learn more about Hawaii, visit ABDO Publishing Company on the World Wide Web. Web site links about Hawaii are featured on our Book Links page. These links are routinely monitored and updated to provide the most current information available.

www.abdopub.com

Index